S0-AZG-251

Summer

Summer

by Alice Low

with pictures by

BEGINNER BOOKS a division of Random House

This title was originally catalogued by the Library of Congress as follows: Low, Alice. Summer. With pictures by Roy McKie. New York, Beginner Books, 1963. 61 p. col. illus. 24 cm. "B-32." 1. Summer—Juvenile literature. i. Title. PZ8.3.L946Su 63-15628 ISBN 0-394-80032-X ISBN 0-394-90032-4 (lib. bdg.)

K   1 2 3 4

We like the things
that summer brings.

It brings the sun.
It brings the heat.
It brings the things
we like to eat.

3

Summer brings
so many things!

It brings us things
to do outside.
It brings new ways
to take a ride.

We like to ride
way out of town.
We like to ride
up hill and down.

It feels so good
when we go fast.
We like to feel
the breeze go past.

We ride and ride
about a mile
and then we stop
and eat a while.
We like cold things.
We eat them up.
And when we eat
so does our pup.

We like the things
that summer brings.

It brings us fireworks
late at night,
all red and yellow,
blue and white.
They go up high.
They are such fun!
Look! Look!
There goes another one.

Some summer days
we take a ride.
The car gets very
hot inside.
And when we sit
in all that heat
we wish that we
had used our feet.

But we don't mind
when it is hot.
Cold water cools us
off a lot.
It cools us off
down to our toes.
Our pup is going
to cool his nose.

Summer brings
so many things.
Summer brings us
rides on swings!

We swing up high
into the trees.
We swing so fast
we make a breeze.

Then down we go
into some hay.
We like to play
this game all day.

Summer brings us things with wings!

We like to catch them

with a net

and see how many

we can get.

Our pup is smart.
Our pup can get
a butterfly
without a net.

And there are days
when our pup finds
some animals
of other kinds.

That animal
is much too near.
Come on! Come on!
Get out of here!

In summer time
we say hello
to all the fish
way down below.

They look at us.

They seem to say,

"What kind of fish

have come our way?"

A summer fair!
A fair is fun!
In summer time
we go to one.
Around, around,
around we go.
The ground is very
far below.

Summer sun
brings garden fun.

We have to water well,
we know,
to make our garden
grow and grow.

You water me.
I water you.
And that will make us
grow fast, too!

34

Some summer nights
we cook and eat.
Our pup is not
so very neat.

We like the things
that summer brings.
We like to fish
with sticks and strings.
We sit and sit.
We wish and wish
that we could catch
just one small fish.

Some days we catch one
ten feet long.
And ten - feet fish
are big and strong.

They get away!
They take our hook.
We never take them
home to cook.

39

One day our pup
got something, too.
But we don't think
he wanted to.

Summer brings
so many things!

On summer nights
we like to be
inside a tent
just right for three.

And picnics are
such fun, you know.
We have them
every day or so.

We like to eat out
under trees.
But so do all
the bugs and bees.

Summer brings
new games to play.
In summer time
we play croquet.

I like
to hit
the ball away.

49

Sometimes I hit
the ball too far,
right in the window
of a car!

We like this way
to spend a day.

We make a sand house
on the shore.
We make some windows
and a door.

Then waves come up.

They come up fast.

Sometimes our sand house

does not last.

But there is lots
of sand to dig
to make another
just as big.

When we go out
on summer nights
we see the fireflies
with their lights.

We catch them.
They will give us light
to find our way
back home at night.

We ask a farmer,
"Will you stop
and let us ride
back home on top?"

We let the fireflies go away.

The moon is out.

It lights our way.

We hear the horse

go clop - clop - clop.

Our pup goes

fast asleep on top.

We stay awake
and think of things . . .
the happy things
that summer brings!

61